Gems from Warren Buffett

D0976359

ALSO BY MARK GAVAGAN

12 Critical Things Your Family Needs to Know

The It's All Right Here Life & Affairs Organizer

These are print/digital workbooks for helping families organize their finances and get their affairs in order, so that if something happens to you, your loved ones will know:

- What you have
- Where it's located, and
- What your wishes are

Learn more at:

www.OrganizeMyAffairs.com

Gems from Warren Buffett

Wit and Wisdom from 34 Years of Letters to Shareholders

By Mark Gavagan

Based upon copyrighted works by Warren Buffett (with permission)

Cole House Productions / Cole House LLC

Table of Contents

To my wife, Kimberly, and our
daughters, Audrey and Sophie

Introduction

The correlation between humor and intelligence is well documented - this book does nothing to dispel that notion regarding Warren Buffett.

It's not an investment tutorial or biography of Mr. Buffett. It's a collection of 240 or so of his wittiest and most insightful thoughts ("gems"), culled from 34 years of his letters to Berkshire Hathaway shareholders.

These gems lighten spirits with their humor, enlighten minds with their wisdom, and provide an interesting view into one of America's most successful and honorable CEOs. Many of these gems have been pulled out of context because their messages are useful well beyond the specific situation for which they were written.

Warren Buffett did not write this book.

All material quoted herein is copyrighted and used with permission of its author, Mr. Buffett.

Obviously most of this book's content was penned by Mr. Buffett. This is part of why 20% of sales are donated to a charity he supports (learn more two pages ahead). I simply read all 400,000 words of his shareholder letters, culled and edited the material into these gems, and added a few comments along the way.

The main reason for so few comments is that Mr. Buffett's material stands on its own.

"America's Funniest Home Videos," the TV series that began in 1990, also served as inspiration. Its entertaining content was constantly interrupted by the hosts' annoying commentary. Here, my annoying commentary is kept to a minimum.

Formatting

Every block quote is from one of Mr. Buffett's letters to Berkshire Hathaway shareholders, with the respective year indicated below each entry (e.g., "-1985 letter" means the quote immediately preceding is from Mr. Buffett's 1985 letter).

Quotes are generally separated by a blank line, followed by three asterisks and another blank line, unless the asterisks would "hang" independently onto the top of a new page, in which case they've been eliminated.

Some of Mr. Buffett's double quotation marks were changed to single ones, because many places where he used them became encapsulated in my quotation of his sentence or paragraph. Thanks to Grammar Girl for help on this topic: http://grammar.quickanddirtytips.com/single-quotes-versus-double-quotes.aspx

20% of Sales Given to Charity

20% of gross sales* from this book will be donated to the GLIDE charity, which Mr. Buffett has generously supported with his own donations. George Costanza's 'Human Fund' was the runner-up.

Gross Sales means the total amount customers pay for the book, not including sales tax collected or shipping (if applicable). No other fees, charges, deductions, expenses or overhead apply - GLIDE gets 20% of the whole enchilada, with no "fuzzy math." Gross sales is a simple, transparent and easily audited figure, so everyone is certain the commitment is fulfilled.

Sales and donation figures will be posted and updated publicly at www.GemsFromBuffett.com.

GLIDE's mission is to create a radically inclusive, just and loving community mobilized to alleviate suffering and break the cycles of poverty and marginalization. GLIDE's methodology is radically simple: love, acceptance, and compassion, which they apply through programs in Wellness, Growth, Spirit, and Leadership.

Visit www.glide.org to learn more.

Managing With Style

On Berkshire's shareholder-oriented management:

> "We are here to make money with you, not off you."

> -1996 letter

* * *

Berkshire's Disgusting "Corporate Bloat"

I love this title, but they actually do run a tight ship...

> "The five people who work here with me ... outproduce corporate groups many times their number. A compact organization lets

all of us spend our time managing the business rather than managing each other."

-1982 letter

* * *

"In a characteristically rash move, we have expanded World Headquarters by 252 square feet (17%)"

-1982 letter

* * *

The Corporate Jet

While notoriously frugal with shareholder funds, particularly regarding executive perks, Mr. Buffett finds the lure of a private corporate jet - thought by some to be a wasteful extravagance - irresistible. That it is so out of character makes Mr. Buffett's humorous disclosures all the more entertaining.

In 1995, Mr. Buffett became a personal customer of what is today called NetJets, the world's largest fractional jet ownership company, which gives individuals and businesses the benefits of whole aircraft ownership at a fraction of the cost. A few years later, Berkshire Hathaway acquired the company and thereabout, sold it's own jet and began relying entirely on NetJets for corporate jet travel.

"Our goal is to do what makes sense for
Berkshire's customers and employees at all
times, and never to add the unneeded. ('But
what about the corporate jet?' you rudely
ask. Well, occasionally a man must rise
above principle.)"

-1987 letter

Readers should understand that Mr. Buffett runs
Berkshire in partnership with his longtime friend, Vice
Chairman Charlie Munger, who is brilliant, shareholder-
minded and perhaps even *more* frugal than Mr. Buffett (he
wasn't a fan of the corporate jet).

This snippet from the 2010 letter conveys the tone of
their relationship: "If you decide to leave (during the
annual shareholder meeting's Q & A), please do so while
Charlie is talking."

"Naming the plane has not been easy. I
initially suggested 'The Charles T. Munger.'
Charlie countered with 'The Aberration.'
We finally settled on 'The Indefensible.' "

-1989 letter

* * *

"My own attitude toward the (new
corporate) jet can be summarized by the
prayer attributed, apocryphally I'm sure, to

St. Augustine as he contemplated leaving a life of secular pleasures to become a priest. Battling the conflict between intellect and glands, he pled: 'Help me, Oh Lord, to become chaste - but not yet.' "

-1989 letter

* * *

"Our entire corporate overhead is less than half the size of our charitable contributions. (Charlie, however, insists that I tell you that $1.4 million of our $4.9 million overhead is attributable to our corporate jet, The Indefensible.)"

-1993 letter

* * *

"Were I to die tomorrow, ... Berkshire's earnings would increase by $1 million annually, since Charlie would immediately sell our corporate jet, The Indefensible (ignoring my wish that it be buried with me)."

-1990 letter

(Note: immediately above is Mark Gavagan's favorite Warren Buffett gem.)

Managing the Managers

Berkshire Hathaway is a holding company, owning part or all of a diverse array of businesses, including insurance companies, railroads, utilities/energy, manufacturing, services, retailing, finance and financial services.

Berkshire's approach is to invest in companies with great businesses AND great management, then mostly leave them alone.

"We possess a cadre of truly skilled managers who have an unusual commitment to their own operations and to Berkshire. Many of our CEOs are independently wealthy and work only because they love what they do. They are volunteers, not mercenaries. Because no one can offer them a job they would enjoy more, they can't be lured away."

-2010 letter

* * *

"We want (CEOs of Berkshire-owned businesses) to feel that the businesses they run are theirs. This means no second-guessing by Charlie and me. We avoid the attitude of the alumnus whose message to the football coach is 'I'm 100% with you -

win or tie.' Our basic goal as an owner is to behave with our managers as we like our owners to behave with us."

-1995 letter

* * *

"At Berkshire, managers can focus on running their businesses: They are not subjected to meetings at headquarters nor financing worries nor Wall Street harassment. They simply get a letter from me every two years ... and call me when they wish. And their wishes do differ: There are managers to whom I have not talked in the last year, while there is one with whom I talk almost daily. Our trust is in people rather than process. A 'hire well, manage little' code suits both them and me.

Berkshire's CEOs come in many forms. Some have MBAs; others never finished college. Some use budgets and are by-the-book types; others operate by the seat of their pants. Our team resembles a baseball squad composed of all-stars having vastly different batting styles. Changes in our line-up are seldom required."

-2010 letter

* * *

On how the managerial stars at Berkshire's operating units, Berkshire's performance is not affected if Charlie or I slip away from time to time (Mr. Buffett was elected Interim Chairman of Salomon Inc. Aug 1990 with no plans to be there permanently):

> "The role that Charlie and I play in the success of our operating units can be illustrated by a story about George Mira, the one-time quarterback of the University of Miami, and his coach, Andy Gustafson. Playing Florida and near its goal line, Mira dropped back to pass. He spotted an open receiver but found his right shoulder in the unshakable grasp of a Florida linebacker. The right-handed Mira thereupon switched the ball to his other hand and threw the only left-handed pass of his life - for a touchdown. As the crowd erupted, Gustafson calmly turned to a reporter and declared: 'Now that's what I call coaching.' "

-1991 letter

* * *

"You learn a great deal about a person when you purchase a business from him and he then stays on to run it as an employee rather than as an owner. Before the purchase the seller knows the business intimately, whereas you start from scratch. The seller has dozens of opportunities to mislead the buyer -

through omissions, ambiguities, and misdirection. After the check has changed hands, subtle (and not so subtle) changes of attitude can occur and implicit understandings can evaporate. As in the courtship-marriage sequence, disappointments are not infrequent."

-1980 letter

* * *

"The attitude of our managers vividly contrasts with that of the young man who married a tycoon's only child, a decidedly homely and dull lass. Relieved, the father called in his new son-in-law after the wedding and began to discuss the future:

'Son, you're the boy I always wanted and never had. Here's a stock certificate for 50% of the company. You're my equal partner from now on.'

'Thanks, dad.'

'Now, what would you like to run? How about sales?'

'I'm afraid I couldn't sell water to a man crawling in the Sahara.'

'Well then, how about heading human relations?'

'I really don't care for people.'

'No problem, we have lots of other spots in the business. What would you like to do?'

'Actually, nothing appeals to me. Why don't you just buy me out?' "

-2005 letter

* * *

"In most cases the remarkable performance of these units arises partially from an exceptional business franchise; in all cases an exceptional management is a vital factor. The contribution Charlie and I make is to leave these managers alone."

-1988 letter

* * *

"Our premium of business value to book value has widened for two simple reasons: We own some remarkable businesses and they are run by even more remarkable managers. You have a right to question that second assertion. After all, CEOs seldom tell their shareholders that they have assembled a bunch of turkeys to run things."

-1987 letter

* * *

"Investors should pay more for a business that is lodged in the hands of a manager with demonstrated pro-shareholder leanings than for one in the hands of a self-interested manager marching to a different drummer."

-1984 letter

* * *

"Irrespective of titles, Charlie and I work as partners in managing all controlled companies. To almost a sinful degree, we enjoy our work as managing partners."

-1981 letter

* * *

"Indeed, if we were not paid at all, Charlie and I would be delighted with the cushy jobs we hold. At bottom, we subscribe to Ronald Reagan's creed: 'It's probably true that hard work never killed anyone, but I figure why take the chance.' "

-1994 letter

* * *

"Last year I stated unequivocally that pre-tax margins at The Buffalo News would fall in 1988. That forecast would have proved correct at almost any other newspaper our size or larger. But (Buffalo News CEO) Stan Lipsey - bless him - has managed to make me look foolish."

-1988 letter

* * *

"Charlie and I put Chuck Huggins in charge of See's (Candies) about five minutes after we bought the company. Upon reviewing his record, you may wonder what took us so long."

-1988 letter

* * *

"A footnote: After our "soft" opening (of a new furniture store for subsidiary R. C. Willey) in August, we had a grand opening of the Boise store about a month later. Naturally, I went there to cut the ribbon (your Chairman, I wish to emphasize, is good for something)."

-1999 letter

* * *

"It's not our style to tamper with successful business cultures (of acquired companies)."

-2001 letter

* * *

"Berkshire's operating CEOs are masters of their crafts and run their businesses as if they were their own. My job is to stay out of their way and allocate whatever excess capital their businesses generate. It's easy work."

-2002 letter

* * *

"There's a reason NetJets (sells and manages fractionally-owned aircraft) is the runaway leader: It offers the ultimate in safety and service. At Berkshire, and at a number of our subsidiaries, NetJets aircraft are an indispensable business tool. I also have a contract for personal use with NetJets and so do members of my family and most Berkshire directors. (None of us, I should add, gets a discount.) Once you've flown NetJets, returning to commercial flights is like going back to holding hands."

-2006 letter

"At 86 and 79, Charlie and I remain lucky beyond our dreams. We were born in America; had terrific parents who saw that we got good educations; have enjoyed wonderful families and great health; and came equipped with a 'business' gene that allows us to prosper in a manner hugely disproportionate to that experienced by many people who contribute as much or more to our society's well-being. Moreover, we have long had jobs that we love, in which we are helped in countless ways by talented and cheerful associates. Indeed, over the years, our work has become ever more fascinating; no wonder we tap-dance to work. If pushed, we would gladly pay substantial sums to have our jobs (but don't tell the Comp Committee)."

-2009 letter

* * *

"Charlie and I believe that those entrusted with handling the funds of others should establish performance goals at the onset of their stewardship. Lacking such standards, managements are tempted to shoot the arrow of performance and then paint the bull's-eye around wherever it lands."

-2010 letter

"Much of the extra value that exists in our businesses has been created by the managers now running them. Charlie and I feel free to brag about this group because we had nothing to do with developing the skills they possess: These superstars just came that way. Our job is merely to identify talented managers and provide an environment in which they can do their stuff."

-1990 letter

* * *

"Accomplishing this will require a few big ideas - small ones just won't do. Charlie Munger, my partner in general management, and I do not have any such ideas at present, but our experience has been that they pop up occasionally. (How's that for a strategic plan?)"

-1984 letter

* * *

"Charlie and I can't promise results, but we do promise you that we will keep our efforts focused on our goals."

-1986 letter

"And now a small hint to Berkshire directors: Last year I spent more than nine times my salary at (Berkshire subsidiaries) Borsheim's and EJA. Just think how Berkshire's business would boom if you'd only spring for a raise."

-1998 letter

* * *

"Ben Graham taught me 45 years ago that in investing it is not necessary to do extraordinary things to get extraordinary results. In later life, I have been surprised to find that this statement holds true in business management as well. What a manager must do is handle the basics well and not get diverted."

-1994 letter

* * *

'Til Death Do Us Part

Warren Buffett turned 81 in August 2011 and Charlie Munger turned 88 in January 2012. Though they've created succession plans, their aim appears to be living and running Berkshire Hathaway forever.

"Berkshire is my first love and one that will never fade: At the Harvard Business School last year, a student asked me when I planned to retire and I replied, 'About five to ten years after I die.' "

-1991 letter

* * *

"Mrs. B (Blumkin), Chairman of Nebraska Furniture Mart, continues at age 93 to outsell and out-hustle any manager I've ever seen. She's at the store seven days a week, from opening to close. Competing with her represents a triumph of courage over judgment.

It's easy to overlook what I consider to be the critical lesson of the Mrs. B saga: at 93, Omaha based Board Chairmen have yet to reach their peak. Please file this fact away to consult before you mark your ballot at the 2024 annual meeting of Berkshire."

-1986 letter

* * *

"Charlie (Munger)'s dictum: 'All I want to know is where I'm going to die so I'll never go there.' "

-1996 letter

* * *

"Whatever the future holds, I make you one promise: I'll keep at least 99% of my net worth in Berkshire for as long as I am around. How long will that be? My model is the loyal Democrat in Fort Wayne who asked to be buried in Chicago so that he could stay active in the party. To that end, I've already selected a "power spot" at the office for my urn."

-1998 letter

* * *

"I've reluctantly discarded the notion of my continuing to manage the portfolio after my death – abandoning my hope to give new meaning to the term 'thinking outside the box.' "

-2007 letter

Honesty, Transparency, Accountability & Accounting

"Candor benefits us as managers: the CEO who misleads others in public may eventually mislead himself in private."

-1983 letter

* * *

"Despite our policy of candor, we will discuss our activities in marketable securities only to the extent legally required. Good investment ideas are rare, valuable and subject to competitive appropriation just as good product or business acquisition ideas are. Therefore, we normally will not talk about our investment ideas."

-1983 letter

* * *

Mr. Buffett has devoted an ocean of ink towards explaining Berkshire's businesses in plain-language detail (both good and bad aspects), so shareholders can understand for themselves what they own and judge how well or poorly the business is being run.

"Segment information is equally essential for investors wanting to know what is going on in a multi-line business. Corporate managers always have insisted upon such information before making acquisition decisions but, until a few years ago, seldom made it available to investors faced with acquisition and disposition decisions of their own. Instead, when owners wishing to understand the economic realities of their business asked for data, managers usually gave them a we-can't-tell-you-what-is-going-on-because-it-would-hurt-the-company answer. Ultimately the SEC ordered disclosure of segment data and management began supplying real answers. The change in their behavior recalls an insight of Al Capone: 'You can get much further with a kind word and a gun than you can with a kind word alone.' "

-1985 letter

* * *

"But facts do not cease to exist, either because they are unpleasant or because they are ignored."

-1981 letter

* * *

"We feel noble intentions should be checked periodically against results."

-1983 letter

* * *

"That does not mean we expect all of our holdings to behave uniformly; some will disappoint us, others will deliver pleasant surprises."

-1983 letter

"John Maynard Keynes said in his masterful The General Theory: 'Worldly wisdom teaches that it is better for reputation to fail conventionally than to succeed unconventionally.' (Or, to put it in less elegant terms, lemmings as a class may be derided but never does an individual lemming get criticized.)"

-2004 letter

* * *

"Accounting numbers, of course, are the language of business and as such are of enormous help to anyone evaluating the worth of a business and tracking its progress. ... Managers and owners need to remember, however, that accounting is but an aid to business thinking, never a substitute for it."

-1986 letter

* * *

"But it's much easier to criticize than to improve such accounting rules. The inherent problems are monumental."

-1980 letter

* * *

On obscure accounting maneuvers that masked significant deterioration in other firms' underlying businesses:

> "The reaction of weak managements to weak operations is often weak accounting. ('It's difficult for an empty sack to stand upright.')"
>
> -1982 letter

* * *

> "You can live a full and rewarding life without ever thinking about Goodwill and its amortization. But students of investment and management should understand the nuances of the subject."
>
> -1983 letter

* * *

> "Questioning GAAP figures may seem impious to some. After all, what are we paying the accountants for if it is not to deliver us the "truth" about our business. But the accountants' job is to record, not to evaluate. The evaluation job falls to investors and managers."
>
> -1986 letter

"We have made a significant accounting change that was mandated for 1988, and likely will have another to make in 1990. When we move figures around from year to year, without any change in economic reality, one of our always-thrilling discussions of accounting is necessary."

-1988 letter

* * *

"Over the years, Charlie and I have observed many accounting-based frauds of staggering size. Few of the perpetrators have been punished; many have not even been censured. It has been far safer to steal large sums with a pen than small sums with a gun."

-1988 letter

* * *

"No financial instrument is evil per se; it's just that some variations have far more potential for mischief than others."

-1989 letter

* * *

"In the long run, of course, trouble awaits managements that paper over operating problems with accounting maneuvers. Eventually, managements of this kind achieve the same result as the seriously-ill patient who tells his doctor: 'I can't afford the operation, but would you accept a small payment to touch up the x-rays?' "

-1991 letter

* * *

"Purchase-price accounting adjustments are ignored for reasons we have explained at length in previous reports and which, as an act of mercy, we won't repeat. (We'll be glad to send masochists the earlier explanations, however.)"

-1995 letter

* * *

"Bad terminology is the enemy of good thinking. When companies or investment professionals use terms such as "EBITDA" and "pro forma," they want you to unthinkingly accept concepts that are dangerously flawed. (In golf, my score is frequently below par on a pro forma basis: I have firm plans to "restructure" my putting stroke and therefore only count the swings I take before reaching the green.)"

-2001 letter

* * *

"Managers that always promise to 'make the numbers' will at some point be tempted to make up the numbers."

-2002 letter

* * *

"The accounting procedure for retroactive transactions is neither well known nor intuitive. The best way for shareholders to understand it, therefore, is for us to simply lay out the debits and credits. Charlie and I would like to see this done more often. We sometimes encounter accounting footnotes about important transactions that leave us baffled, and we go away suspicious that the reporting company wished it that way. (For example, try comprehending transactions "described" in the old 10-Ks of Enron, even after you know how the movie ended.)"

-2006 letter

* * *

"A small chance of distress or disgrace cannot, in our view, be offset by a large chance of extra returns. If your actions are sensible, you are certain to get good results; in most such cases, leverage just moves things along faster. Charlie and I have never been in a big hurry: We enjoy the process far more than the proceeds - though we have learned to live with those also."

-1989 letter

* * *

"Funny business in accounting is not new."

-1990 letter

* * *

"...earnings can be as pliable as putty when a charlatan heads the company reporting them. Eventually truth will surface, but in the meantime a lot of money can change hands. Indeed, some important American fortunes have been created by the monetization of accounting mirages."

-1990 letter

* * *

I Screwed Up

"I would like to tell you that the mistakes I will describe originated with Charlie. But whenever I try to explain things that way, my nose begins to grow."

-1994 letter

* * *

"However, the mild degree of caution that we exercised was an improper response to the world unfolding about us. You do not adequately protect yourself by being half awake while others are sleeping."

-1979 letter

* * *

"We should have realized the futility of trying to be very clever ... in an area where the tide was running heavily against us."

-1979 letter

"Our preaching was better than our performance. (We neglected the Noah principle: predicting rain doesn't count, building arks does.)"

-1981 letter

* * *

"I ignored Comte's advice - 'the intellect should be the servant of the heart, but not its slave' - and believed what I preferred to believe."

-1985 letter

* * *

"We should do well in several segments of our insurance business. Mike Goldberg has made many important improvements in the operation (prior mismanagement by your Chairman having provided him ample opportunity to do so)."

-1985 letter

* * *

"It's a good idea to review past mistakes before committing new ones. So let's take a quick look at the last 25 years."

-1989 letter

"We feel much better about our USAir preferred (an investment holding) than we did a year ago, but your guess is as good as mine as to its ultimate value. (Indeed, considering my record with this investment, it's fair to say that your guess may be better than mine.)"

-1995 letter

* * *

"I try to look out ten or twenty years when making an acquisition, but sometimes my eyesight has been poor."

-2010 letter

* * *

"The figures show the amount of error in our yearend 1985 liabilities that a year of settlements and further evaluation has revealed. As you can see, what I told you last year about our loss liabilities was far from true - and that makes three years in a row of error. If the physiological rules that applied to Pinocchio were to apply to me, my nose would now draw crowds."

-1986 letter

Seeking Long-Term Shareholder Partners (Only)

Mr. Buffett is famously disdainful of short-term shareholders (and investments).

"If the holders of a company's stock and/or the prospective buyers attracted to it are prone to make irrational or emotion-based decisions, some pretty silly stock prices are going to appear periodically. Manic-depressive personalities produce manic-depressive valuations. Such aberrations may help us in buying and selling the stocks of other companies."

-1983 letter

His argument against splitting Berkshire's stock (a stock split divides each share into a multiple lower-priced shares, but does nothing to change the value of the underlying business):

> "Could we really improve our shareholder group by trading some of our present clear-thinking members for impressionable new ones who, preferring paper to value, feel wealthier with nine $10 bills than with one $100 bill?"
>
> -1983 letter

* * *

> "In large part, companies obtain the shareholder constituency that they seek and deserve. If they focus their thinking and communications on short-term results or short-term stock market consequences they will, in large part, attract shareholders who focus on the same factors ... You can't be all things to all men, simultaneously seeking different owners whose primary interests run from high current yield to long-term capital growth to stock market pyrotechnics, etc.
>
> The reasoning of managements that seek large trading activity in their shares puzzles us. In effect, such managements are saying that they want a good many of the existing

clientele continually to desert them in favor of new ones - because you can't add lots of new owners (with new expectations) without losing lots of former owners.

We much prefer owners who like our service and menu and who return year after year. It would be hard to find a better group to sit in the Berkshire Hathaway shareholder "seats" than those already occupying them. So we hope to continue to have a very low turnover among our owners, reflecting a constituency that understands our operation, approves of our policies, and shares our expectations. And we hope to deliver on those expectations."

-1979 letter

* * *

"According the name "investors" to institutions that trade actively is like calling someone who repeatedly engages in one-night stands a romantic."

-1991 letter

Smart Business

"One of the lessons your management has learned - and, unfortunately, sometimes re-learned - is the importance of being in businesses where tailwinds prevail rather than headwinds."

-1977 letter

* * *

"Overall, we opt for Polonius (slightly restated): 'Neither a short-term borrower nor a long-term lender be.' "

-1979 letter

* * *

"In the end, major additional investment in a terrible industry usually is about as rewarding as struggling in quicksand."

-1983 letter

On See's Candy Shops:

> "In effect, raw material costs are largely beyond our control since we will, as a matter of course, buy the finest ingredients that we can, regardless of changes in their price levels. We regard product quality as sacred."

-1983 letter

* * *

> "Price and value can differ; price is what you give, value is what you get."

-1983 letter

* * *

> "Mrs. B (Rose Blumkin) boils it down to 'sell cheap and tell the truth' "

-1984 letter

* * *

> "Who says "you can't lose 'em all"?"

-1984 letter

* * *

"No matter how attractive the prospects of their business. We've never succeeded in making a good deal with a bad person."

-1989 letter

* * *

"We've always found a telephone call to be more productive than a half-day committee meeting."

-1982 letter

* * *

"Our view, we warn you, is non-conventional."

-1980 letter

* * *

"Our gain in net worth during the year was $613.6 million, or 48.2%. It is fitting that the visit of Halley's Comet coincided with this percentage gain: neither will be seen again in my lifetime."

-1985 letter

* * *

"An iron law of business is that growth eventually dampens exceptional economics."

-1985

* * *

"Economic gains must be evaluated by comparison with the capital that produces them."

-1984 letter

* * *

"As our history indicates, we are comfortable both with total ownership of businesses and with marketable securities representing small portions of businesses. We continually look for ways to employ large sums in each area. (But we try to avoid small commitments - 'If something's not worth doing at all, it's not worth doing well.')"

-1981 letter

* * *

"This devastating outcome for the shareholders indicates what can happen when much brain power and energy are applied to a faulty premise. The situation is suggestive of Samuel Johnson's horse: 'A horse that can count to ten is a remarkable horse - not a remarkable mathematician.' Likewise, a textile company that allocates capital brilliantly within its industry is a remarkable textile company - but not a remarkable business."

-1985 letter

* * *

"My conclusion from my own experiences and from much observation of other businesses is that a good managerial record (measured by economic returns) is far more a function of what business boat you get into than it is of how effectively you row (though intelligence and effort help considerably, of course, in any business, good or bad). Some years ago I wrote: 'When a management with a reputation for brilliance tackles a business with a reputation for poor fundamental economics, it is the reputation of the business that remains intact.' Nothing has since changed my point of view on that matter. Should you find yourself in a chronically-leaking boat, energy devoted to changing vessels is likely to be more productive than energy devoted to patching leaks."

-1985 letter

"We neither understand the adding of unneeded people or activities because profits are booming, nor the cutting of essential people or activities because profitability is shrinking. That kind of yo-yo approach is neither business-like nor humane."

-1987 letter

* * *

On estimating past versus future business value:

"The rear-view mirror is one thing; the windshield is another."

-1989 letter

* * *

"Capital outlays at a business can be skipped, of course, in any given month, just as a human can skip a day or even a week of eating. But if the skipping becomes routine and is not made up, the body weakens and eventually dies. Furthermore, a start-and-stop feeding policy will over time produce a less healthy organism, human or corporate, than that produced by a steady diet. As businessmen, Charlie and I relish having competitors who are unable to fund capital expenditures."

-1989 letter

"Five years ago we had no thought of getting into shoes. Now we have 7,200 employees in that industry, and I sing 'There's No Business Like Shoe Business' as I drive to work. So much for strategic plans.

At Berkshire, we have no view of the future that dictates what businesses or industries we will enter. Indeed, we think it's usually poison for a corporate giant's shareholders if it embarks upon new ventures pursuant to some grand vision. We prefer instead to focus on the economic characteristics of businesses that we wish to own and the personal characteristics of managers with whom we wish to associate - and then to hope we get lucky in finding the two in combination."

-1993 letter

* * *

"In 1994, Coca-Cola sold about 280 billion 8-ounce servings and earned a little less than a penny on each. But pennies add up."

-1994 letter

* * *

On owning minority shares in another company:

"It's far better to own a significant portion of the Hope diamond than 100% of a rhinestone"

-1994 letter

* * *

"R.C. Willey is an amazing story. Bill took over the business from his father-in-law in 1954 when sales were about $250,000. From this tiny base, Bill employed Mae West's philosophy: 'It's not what you've got - it's what you do with what you've got.' "

-1995 letter

* * *

" In business, I look for economic castles protected by unbreachable 'moats.' "

-1995 letter

* * *

"(By the year 2021), I wouldn't be surprised to see our share of Coke's annual earnings exceed 100% of what we paid for the investment. Time is the friend of the wonderful business."

-2010 letter

"(New Berkshire investment manager Todd Combs) will be paid a salary plus a contingent payment based on his performance relative to the S&P. Todd initially will manage funds in the range of one to three billion dollars, an amount he can reset annually. His focus will be equities but he is not restricted to that form of investment. (Fund consultants like to require style boxes such as "long-short," "macro," "international equities." At Berkshire our only style box is "smart.")"

-2010 letter

* * *

"I won't close down businesses of sub-normal profitability merely to add a fraction of a point to our corporate rate of return. However, I also feel it inappropriate for even an exceptionally profitable company to fund an operation once it appears to have unending losses in prospect."

-1985 letter

* * *

"Good jockeys will do well on good horses, but not on broken-down nags."

-1989 letter

* * *

"...value is in no way affected by the inclusion or non-inclusion of those retained earnings in our own reported operating earnings. If a tree grows in a forest partially owned by us, but we don't record the growth in our financial statements, we still own part of the tree."

-1980 letter

* * *

The Insurance Business

"Finally, some ('super-catastrophic' insurance policies Berkshire writes) are triggered only by a catastrophe of a specific type, such as an earthquake. Our exposures are large: We have one policy that calls for us to pay $100 million to the policyholder if a specified catastrophe occurs. (Now you know why I suffer eyestrain: from watching The Weather Channel.)"

-1992 letter

On 1994 California Northridge earthquake losses:

> "...The Northridge quake of 1994 laid
> homeowners' losses on insurers that greatly
> exceeded what computer models had told
> them to expect. Yet the intensity of that
> quake was mild compared to the 'worst-case'
> possibility for California. Understandably,
> insurers became - ahem - shaken and started
> contemplating a retreat from writing
> earthquake coverage into their homeowners'
> policies."

-1996 letter

* * *

> "One thing, though, we have learned – the
> hard way – after many years in the business:
> Surprises in insurance are far from
> symmetrical. You are lucky if you get one
> that is pleasant for every ten that go the
> other way. Too often, however, insurers react
> to looming loss problems with optimism.
> They behave like the fellow in a switchblade
> fight who, after his opponent has taken a
> mighty swipe at his throat, exclaimed, 'You
> never touched me.' His adversary's reply:
> 'Just wait until you try to shake your head.' "

-2005 letter

* * *

"We would rather have some slack in the organization (i.e., too many insurance employees for the current business volume) from time to time than keep everyone terribly busy writing business on which we are going to lose money."

-1979 letter

* * *

"I heard a story recently that is applicable to our insurance accounting problems: a man was traveling abroad when he received a call from his sister informing him that their father had died unexpectedly. It was physically impossible for the brother to get back home for the funeral, but he told his sister to take care of the funeral arrangements and to send the bill to him. After returning home he received a bill for several thousand dollars, which he promptly paid. The following month another bill came along for $15, and he paid that too. Another month followed, with a similar bill. When, in the next month, a third bill for $15 was presented, he called his sister to ask what was going on. "Oh", she said. "I forgot to tell you. We buried Dad in a rented suit.

If you've been in the insurance business in recent years - particularly the reinsurance

business - this story hurts. We have tried to
include all of our "rented suit" liabilities in
our current financial statement, but our
record of past error should make us humble,
and you suspicious. I will continue to report
to you the errors, plus or minus, that surface
each year."

-1984 letter

* * *

"When shortages exist, however, even
commodity businesses flourish. The
insurance industry enjoyed that kind of
climate for a while but it is now gone. One
of the ironies of capitalism is that most
managers in commodity industries abhor
shortage conditions - even though those are
the only circumstances permitting them
good returns. Whenever shortages appear,
the typical manager simply can't wait to
expand capacity and thereby plug the hole
through which money is showering upon
him."

-1987 letter

* * *

"(Other insurance companies) do not want to expose themselves to an embarrassing single-quarter loss, even if the managerial strategy that causes the loss promises, over time, to produce superior results. I can understand their thinking: What is best for their owners is not necessarily best for the managers. Fortunately Charlie and I have both total job security and financial interests that are identical with those of our shareholders. We are willing to look foolish as long as we don't feel we have acted foolishly."

-1989 letter

* * *

"Despite the difficulties we have had in reserving and the commodity economics of the (insurance) industry, we expect our insurance business to both grow and make significant amounts of money - but progress will be distinctly irregular and there will be major unpleasant surprises from time to time. It's a treacherous business and a wary attitude is essential. We must heed Woody Allen: 'While the lamb may lie down with the lion, the lamb shouldn't count on getting a whole lot of sleep.' "

-1986 letter

"Our insurance volume over the next few years is likely to run very low, since business with a reasonable potential for profit will almost certainly be scarce. So be it. At Berkshire, we simply will not write policies at rates that carry the expectation of economic loss. We encounter enough troubles when we expect a gain. ... At some point - we don't know when - we will be deluged with insurance business. The cause will probably be some major physical or financial catastrophe. But we could also experience an explosion in business, as we did in 1985, because large and increasing underwriting losses at other companies coincide with their recognition that they are far underreserved. in the meantime, we will retain our talented professionals, protect our capital, and try not to make major mistakes."

-1988 letter

* * *

The Airline Industry

"It should be no surprise to anyone that those airline employees who contractually receive above-market salaries will resist any reduction in these as long as their checks continue to clear"

-1994 letter

* * *

"When Richard Branson, the wealthy owner of Virgin Atlantic Airways, was asked how to become a millionaire, he had a quick answer: 'There's really nothing to it. Start as a billionaire and then buy an airline.' "

-1996 letter

Acquisitions &

Investments

"The market, like the Lord, helps those who help themselves. But, unlike the Lord, the market does not forgive those who know not what they do. For the investor, a too-high purchase price for the stock of an excellent company can undo the effects of a subsequent decade of favorable business developments."

-1982 letter

* * *

"What really makes us dance is the purchase of 100% of good businesses at reasonable prices ... but it is an extraordinarily difficult job..."

-1982 letter

"As we look at the major acquisitions that others made during 1982, our reaction is not envy, but relief that we were non-participants. For in many of these acquisitions, managerial intellect wilted in competition with managerial adrenaline. The thrill of the chase blinded the pursuers to the consequences of the catch. Pascal's observation seems apt: "It has struck me that all men's misfortunes spring from the single cause that they are unable to stay quietly in one room.""

-1982 letter

* * *

"Managers with bright, but adrenaline-soaked minds scramble after foolish acquisitions..."

-1983 letter

* * *

"One question I always ask myself in appraising a business is how I would like, assuming I had ample capital and skilled personnel, to compete with it."

-1983 letter

* * *

On synergy:

> "… a term widely used in business to explain an acquisition that otherwise makes no sense."

> -1985 letter

* * *

> "We try to buy into businesses with favorable long-term economics. Our goal is to find an outstanding business at a sensible price, not a mediocre business at a bargain price. Charlie and I have found that making silk purses out of silk is the best that we can do; with sow's ears, we fail."

> -1987 letter

* * *

On their ongoing efforts to acquire businesses with excellent economic characteristics and a management they like, trust and admire:

> "Such acquisitions are not easy to make but we look for them constantly. In the search, we adopt the same attitude one might find appropriate in looking for a spouse: It pays to be active, interested and open-minded, but it does not pay to be in a hurry."

> -1992 letter

"If a business is attractive enough to buy once, it may well pay to repeat the process. We would love to increase our economic interest in See's or Scott Fetzer, but we haven't found a way to add to a 100% holding."

-1994 letter

* * *

"We believe most deals do damage to the shareholders of the acquiring company. Too often, the words from HMS Pinafore apply: 'Things are seldom what they seem, skim milk masquerades as cream.' Specifically, sellers and their representatives invariably present financial projections having more entertainment value than educational value. In the production of rosy scenarios, Wall Street can hold its own against Washington.

In any case, why potential buyers even look at projections prepared by sellers baffles me. Charlie and I never give them a glance, but instead keep in mind the story of the man with an ailing horse. Visiting the vet, he said: 'Can you help me? Sometimes my horse walks just fine and sometimes he limps.' The vet's reply was pointed: 'No

problem - when he's walking fine, sell him.'
In the world of mergers and acquisitions,
that horse would be peddled as Secretariat."

-1995 letter

* * *

"Charlie and I bring a modicum of product
expertise to this (acquisition of International
Dairy Queen): He has been patronizing the
Dairy Queens in Cass Lake and Bemidji,
Minnesota, for decades, and I have been a
regular in Omaha. We have put our money
where our mouth is."

-1997 letter

* * *

"If a CEO is enthused about a particularly
foolish acquisition, both his internal staff
and his outside advisors will come up with
whatever projections are needed to justify his
stance. Only in fairy tales are emperors told
that they are naked."

-1997 letter

* * *

"At yearend, we held more than $15 billion in cash equivalents (including high-grade securities due in less than one year). Cash never makes us happy. But it's better to have the money burning a hole in Berkshire's pocket than resting comfortably in someone else's."

-1998 letter

* * *

"I will detail our (acquisition) purchases in the next section of the report. But I will tell you now that we have embraced the 21st century by entering such cutting-edge industries as brick, carpet, insulation and paint. Try to control your excitement."

-2000 letter

* * *

After buying Shaw Industries, the world's largest carpet manufacturer:

"Now, if people walk all over us, we won't mind."

-2000 letter

* * *

"Unlike many business buyers, Berkshire has no "exit strategy." We buy to keep. We do, though, have an entrance strategy, looking for businesses in this country or abroad that meet our six criteria and are available at a price that will produce a reasonable return. If you have a business that fits, give me a call. Like a hopeful teenage girl, I'll be waiting by the phone."

-2005 letter

* * *

"We continue, however, to need "elephants" in order for us to use Berkshire's flood of incoming cash. Charlie and I must therefore ignore the pursuit of mice and focus our acquisition efforts on much bigger game.

Our exemplar is the older man who crashed his grocery cart into that of a much younger fellow while both were shopping. The elderly man explained apologetically that he had lost track of his wife and was preoccupied searching for her. His new acquaintance said that by coincidence his wife had also wandered off and suggested that it might be more efficient if they jointly looked for the two women. Agreeing, the older man asked his new companion what his wife looked like. 'She's a gorgeous blonde,' the fellow answered, 'with a body that would cause a bishop to go through a stained glass window, and she's wearing tight white shorts. How about yours?' The senior citizen wasted no words: 'Forget her, we'll look for yours.' "

-2006 letter

* * *

"Long ago, Ben Graham taught me that 'price is what you pay; value is what you get.' "

-2008 letter

* * *

"Berkshire acquired GEICO in two stages. In 1976-80 we bought about one-third of the company's stock for $47 million. Over the years, large repurchases by the company of its own shares caused our position to grow to about 50% without our having bought any more shares. Then, on January 2, 1996, we acquired the remaining 50% of GEICO for $2.3 billion in cash, about 50 times the cost of our original purchase.

An old Wall Street joke gets close to our experience:

Customer: Thanks for putting me in XYZ stock at 5. I hear it's up to 18.

Broker: Yes, and that's just the beginning. In fact, the company is doing so well now, that it's an even better buy at 18 than it was when you made your purchase.

Customer: Damn, I knew I should have waited."

-2009 letter

* * *

"Big opportunities come infrequently. When it's raining gold, reach for a bucket, not a thimble."

-2009 letter

* * *

"Charlie and I enjoy issuing Berkshire stock (for acquisitions) about as much as we relish prepping for a colonoscopy."

-2009 letter

* * *

"In selecting common stocks, we devote our attention to attractive purchases, not to the possibility of attractive sales."

-1985 letter

"Currently liking neither stocks nor bonds, I find myself the polar opposite of Mae West as she declared: 'I like only two kinds of men - foreign and domestic.' "

-1986 letter

* * *

"So our main capital allocation moves in 1986 were to pay off debt and stockpile funds. Neither is a fate worse than death, but they do not inspire us to do handsprings either."

-1986 letter

* * *

"We prefer, of course, to make major long-term commitments, but we often have more cash than good ideas."

-1988 letter

* * *

"Bonds are no better than the currency in which they are denominated"

-1987 letter

* * *

"I find it uncomfortable when friends or acquaintances mention that they are buying X because it has been reported - incorrectly - that Berkshire is a buyer. However, I do not set them straight. If they want to participate in whatever Berkshire actually is buying, they can always purchase Berkshire stock. But perhaps that is too simple. Usually, I suspect, they find it more exciting to buy what is being talked about. Whether that strategy is more profitable is another question."

-1987 letter

* * *

"I believe I had my first Coca-Cola in either 1935 or 1936. Of a certainty, it was in 1936 that I started buying Cokes at the rate of six for 25 cents from Buffett & Son, the family grocery store, to sell around the neighborhood for 5 cents each. In this excursion into high-margin retailing, I duly observed the extraordinary consumer attractiveness and commercial possibilities of the product."

-1989 letter

* * *

"Berkshire's past rates of gain in both book value and business value were achieved under circumstances far different from those that now exist. Anyone ignoring these differences makes the same mistake that a baseball manager would were he to judge the future prospects of a 42-year-old center fielder on the basis of his lifetime batting average."

-1988 letter

* * *

"Lethargy bordering on sloth remains the cornerstone of our investment style: This year we neither bought nor sold a share of five of our six major holdings."

-1990 letter

* * *

"Stocks cannot forever overperform their underlying businesses, as they have so dramatically done for some time."

-1992 letter

* * *

"I find that a long-term familiarity with a company and its products is often helpful in evaluating it."

-1994 letter

* * *

"Our future rates of gain will fall far short of those achieved in the past. Berkshire's capital base is now simply too large to allow us to earn truly outsized returns. If you believe otherwise, you should consider a career in sales but avoid one in mathematics (bearing in mind that there are really only three kinds of people in the world: those who can count and those who can't)."

-1998 letter

* * *

"Our acquisition decisions will be aimed at maximizing real economic benefits, not at maximizing either managerial domain or reported numbers for accounting purposes. (In the long run, managements stressing accounting appearance over economic substance usually achieve little of either.)"

-1981 letter

Bankers, Brokers, Consultants and other "Helpers"

"In the securities business, whatever can be sold will be sold."

-1996 letter

* * *

" 'Forecasts', said Sam Goldwyn, 'are dangerous, particularly those about the future.' "

-1981 letter

"It's not only generals that prefer to fight the last war. Most business and investment analysis also comes from the rear-view mirror."

-1982 letter

* * *

"Several times since, we have seen John (Gutfreund, CEO of Salomon Inc.) steer clients away from transactions that would have been unwise, but that the client clearly wanted to make - even though his advice provided no fee to Salomon and acquiescence would have delivered a large fee. Such service-above-self behavior is far from automatic in Wall Street."

-1987 letter

* * *

"Wall Street welcomed this invention with the enthusiasm less-enlightened folk might reserve for the wheel or the plow. Here (in questionable but aggressively promoted zero-coupon or PIK bonds), finally, was an instrument that would let the Street make deals at prices no longer limited by actual earning power. The result, obviously, would be more transactions: Silly prices will always attract sellers. And, as Jesse Unruh might have put it, transactions are the mother's milk of finance.

The zero-coupon or PIK bond possesses one additional attraction for the promoter and investment banker, which is that the time elapsing between folly and failure can be stretched out. This is no small benefit. If the period before all costs must be faced is long, promoters can create a string of foolish deals - and take in lots of fees - before any chickens come home to roost from their earlier ventures.

But in the end, alchemy, whether it is metallurgical or financial, fails. A base business can not be transformed into a golden business by tricks of accounting or capital structure. The man claiming to be a financial alchemist may become rich. But gullible investors rather than business achievements will usually be the source of his wealth."

-1989 letter

* * *

"Our comments about investment bankers may seem harsh. But Charlie and I - in our hopelessly old-fashioned way - believe that they should perform a gatekeeping role, guarding investors against the promoter's propensity to indulge in excess. Promoters, after all, have throughout time exercised the same judgment and restraint in accepting money that alcoholics have exercised in accepting liquor. At a minimum, therefore, the banker's conduct should rise to that of a responsible bartender who, when necessary, refuses the profit from the next drink to avoid sending a drunk out on the highway. In recent years, unfortunately, many leading investment firms have found bartender morality to be an intolerably restrictive standard. Lately, those who have traveled the high road in Wall Street have not encountered heavy traffic."

-1989 letter

* * *

"Often, much of the pressure (to execute a transaction) comes from brokers whose compensation is contingent upon consummation of a sale, regardless of its consequences for both buyer and seller."

-1990 letter

* * *

"Such high-rate reborrowing schemes, which a few years ago were appropriately confined to the waterfront, soon became models of modern finance at virtually all major investment banking houses.

When they make these offerings, investment bankers display their humorous side: They dispense income and balance sheet projections extending five or more years into the future for companies they barely had heard of a few months earlier. If you are shown such schedules, I suggest that you join in the fun: Ask the investment banker for the one-year budgets that his own firm prepared as the last few years began and then compare these with what actually happened."

-1989 letter

* * *

"The only value of stock forecasters is to make fortune tellers look good."

-1992 letter

* * *

"The blue ribbon for mischief-making should go to the zero-coupon issuer unable to make its interest payments on a current basis. Our advice: Whenever an investment banker starts talking about EBDIT - or whenever someone creates a capital structure that does not allow all interest, both payable and accrued, to be comfortably met out of current cash flow net of ample capital expenditures - zip up your wallet. Turn the tables by suggesting that the promoter and his high-priced entourage accept zero-coupon fees, deferring their take until the zero-coupon bonds have been paid in full. See then how much enthusiasm for the deal endures."

-1989 letter

* * *

"Clearly the attitude of disrespect that many executives have today for accurate reporting is a business disgrace. And auditors, as we have already suggested, have done little on the positive side. Though auditors should regard the investing public as their client, they tend to kowtow instead to the managers who choose them and dole out their pay."

-1998 letter

* * *

"But a pin lies in wait for every bubble. And when the two eventually meet, a new wave of investors learns some very old lessons: First, many in Wall Street - a community in which quality control is not prized - will sell investors anything they will buy. Second, speculation is most dangerous when it looks easiest."

-2000 letter

* * *

"Investment managers often profit far more from piling up assets than from handling those assets well. So when one tells you that increased funds won't hurt his investment performance, step back: His nose is about to grow."

-2003 letter

* * *

"When Walter and Edwin (Schloss) were asked in 1989 by Outstanding Investors Digest, 'How would you summarize your approach?' Edwin replied, 'We try to buy stocks cheap.' So much for Modern Portfolio Theory, technical analysis, macroeconomic thoughts and complex algorithms."

-2006 letter

"Investors should be skeptical of history-based models. Constructed by a nerdy-sounding priesthood using esoteric terms such as beta, gamma, sigma and the like, these models tend to look impressive. Too often, though, investors forget to examine the assumptions behind the symbols. Our advice: Beware of geeks bearing formulas."

-2008 letter

* * *

"The hedge-fund world has witnessed some terrible behavior by general partners who have received huge payouts on the upside and who then, when bad results occurred, have walked away rich, with their limited partners losing back their earlier gains. Sometimes these same general partners thereafter quickly started another fund so that they could immediately participate in future profits without having to overcome their past losses. Investors who put money with such managers should be labeled patsies, not partners."

-2010 letter

* * *

"Part of the appeal of Black-Scholes to auditors and regulators is that it produces a precise number. Charlie and I can't supply one of those. We believe the true liability of our contracts to be far lower than that calculated by Black-Scholes, but we can't come up with an exact figure – anymore than we can come up with a precise value for GEICO, BNSF, or for Berkshire Hathaway itself. Our inability to pinpoint a number doesn't bother us: We would rather be approximately right than precisely wrong."

-2010 letter

* * *

"You can be highly successful as an investor without having the slightest ability to value an option. What students should be learning is how to value a business. That's what investing is all about."

-2010 letter

* * *

"Almost by definition, a really good business generates far more money (at least after its early years) than it can use internally. The company could, of course, distribute the money to shareholders by way of dividends or share repurchases. But often the CEO asks a strategic planning staff, consultants or investment bankers whether an acquisition or two might make sense. That's like asking your interior decorator whether you need a $50,000 rug."

-1994 letter

* * *

"We purchased several companies whose earnings will almost certainly decline this year from peaks they reached in 1999 or 2000. The declines make no difference to us, given that we expect all of our businesses to now and then have ups and downs. (Only in the sales presentations of investment banks do earnings move forever upward.)"

-2000 letter

* * *

"As long as major investors willingly don their Peter Pan wings and repeatedly say 'I believe,' there is no limit to how much 'income' can be created by the zero-coupon bond."

-1989 letter

"The banking business is no favorite of ours. When assets are twenty times equity - a common ratio in this industry - mistakes that involve only a small portion of assets can destroy a major portion of equity. And mistakes have been the rule rather than the exception at many major banks. Most have resulted from a managerial failing that we described last year when discussing the 'institutional imperative:' the tendency of executives to mindlessly imitate the behavior of their peers, no matter how foolish it may be to do so. In their lending, many bankers played follow-the-leader with lemming-like zeal; now they are experiencing a lemming-like fate."

-1990 letter

* * *

"But as happens in Wall Street all too often, what the wise do in the beginning, fools do in the end. In the last few years zero-coupon bonds (and their functional equivalent, pay-in-kind bonds, which distribute additional PIK bonds semi-annually as interest instead of paying cash) have been issued in enormous quantities by ever-junkier credits. To these issuers, zero (or PIK) bonds offer one overwhelming advantage: It is impossible to default on a promise to pay nothing. Indeed, if LDC governments had issued no debt in the 1970's other than long-term zero-coupon obligations, they would now have a spotless record as debtors.

This principle at work - that you need not default for a long time if you solemnly promise to pay nothing for a long time - has not been lost on promoters and investment bankers seeking to finance ever-shakier deals. But its acceptance by lenders took a while: When the leveraged buy-out craze began some years back, purchasers could borrow only on a reasonably sound basis, in which conservatively-estimated free cash flow - that is, operating earnings plus depreciation and amortization less normalized capital expenditures - was adequate to cover both interest and modest reductions in debt.

Later, as the adrenalin of deal-makers surged, businesses began to be purchased at prices so high that all free cash flow necessarily had to be allocated to the payment of interest. That left nothing for the paydown of debt. In effect, a Scarlett O'Hara 'I'll think about it tomorrow' position in respect to principal payments was taken by borrowers and accepted by a new breed of lender, the buyer of original-issue junk bonds. Debt now became something to be refinanced rather than repaid. The change brings to mind a New Yorker cartoon in which the grateful borrower rises to shake the hand of the bank's lending officer and gushes: 'I don't know how I'll ever repay you.' "

-1989 letter

* * *

"You might think that waving away a major expense such as depreciation in an attempt to make a terrible deal look like a good one hits the limits of Wall Street's ingenuity. If so, you haven't been paying attention during the past few years. Promoters needed to find a way to justify even pricier acquisitions. Otherwise, they risked - heaven forbid! - losing deals to other promoters with more 'imagination.' "

-1989 letter

* * *

"One distressing footnote: The cost of the zero-coupon folly will not be borne solely by the direct participants. Certain savings and loan associations were heavy buyers of such bonds, using cash that came from FSLIC-insured deposits. Straining to show splendid earnings, these buyers recorded - but did not receive - ultra-high interest income on these issues. Many of these associations are now in major trouble. Had their loans to shaky credits worked, the owners of the associations would have pocketed the profits. In the many cases in which the loans will fail, the taxpayer will pick up the bill. To paraphrase Jackie Mason, at these associations it was the managers who should have been wearing the ski masks. "

-1989 letter

Market Forces: Fear, Greed, Risk and Reward

"Occasional outbreaks of those two super-contagious diseases, fear and greed, will forever occur in the investment community. The timing of these epidemics will be unpredictable. And the market aberrations produced by them will be equally unpredictable, both as to duration and degree. Therefore, we never try to anticipate the arrival or departure of either disease. Our goal is more modest: we simply attempt to be fearful when others are greedy and to be greedy only when others are fearful."

-1986 letter

"We have never attempted to forecast what the stock market is going to do in the next month or the next year, and we are not trying to do that now. But, as I point out in the enclosed article, equity investors currently seem wildly optimistic in their expectations about future returns."

-1999 letter

* * *

"As this is written, little fear is visible in Wall Street. Instead, euphoria prevails - and why not? What could be more exhilarating than to participate in a bull market in which the rewards to owners of businesses become gloriously uncoupled from the plodding performances of the businesses themselves. Unfortunately, however, stocks can't outperform businesses indefinitely.

Indeed, because of the heavy transaction and investment management costs they bear, stockholders as a whole and over the long term must inevitably underperform the companies they own. If American business, in aggregate, earns about 12% on equity annually, investors must end up earning significantly less. Bull markets can obscure mathematical laws, but they cannot repeal them."

-1986 letter

"Management cannot determine market prices, although it can, by its disclosures and policies, encourage rational behavior by market participants. My own preference, as perhaps you'd guess, is for a market price that consistently approximates business value. Given that relationship, all owners prosper precisely as the business prospers during their period of ownership. Wild swings in market prices far above and below business value do not change the final gains for owners in aggregate; in the end, investor gains must equal business gains. But long periods of substantial undervaluation and/ or overvaluation will cause the gains of the business to be inequitably distributed among various owners, with the investment result of any given owner largely depending upon how lucky, shrewd, or foolish he happens to be."

-1985 letter

* * *

"Despite three years of falling prices, which have significantly improved the attractiveness of common stocks, we still find very few that even mildly interest us. That dismal fact is testimony to the insanity of valuations reached during The Great Bubble. Unfortunately, the hangover may prove to be proportional to the binge."

-2002 letter

* * *

"When we can't find anything exciting in which to invest, our 'default' position is U.S. Treasuries, both bills and repos. No matter how low the yields on these instruments go, we never 'reach' for a little more income by dropping our credit standards or by extending maturities. Charlie and I detest taking even small risks unless we feel we are being adequately compensated for doing so. About as far as we will go down that path is to occasionally eat cottage cheese a day after the expiration date on the carton."

-2003 letter

* * *

"When forced to choose, I will not trade even a night's sleep for the chance of extra profits."

-2008 letter

* * *

"Some major financial institutions have, however, experienced staggering problems because they engaged in the 'weakened lending practices' I described in last year's letter. John Stumpf, CEO of Wells Fargo, aptly dissected the recent behavior of many lenders: 'It is interesting that the industry has invented new ways to lose money when the old ways seemed to work just fine.' "

-2007 letter

* * *

"We have no idea how long the excesses will last, nor do we know what will change the attitudes of government, lender and buyer that fuel them. But we do know that the less the prudence with which others conduct their affairs, the greater the prudence with which we should conduct our own affairs. We have no desire to arbitrage transactions that reflect the unbridled - and, in our view, often unwarranted - optimism of both buyers and lenders. In our activities, we will heed the wisdom of Herb Stein: 'If something can't go on forever, it will end.' "

-1988 letter

* * *

Government

"Government has been exceptionally able in printing money and creating promises, but is unable to print gold or create oil."

-1979 letter

* * *

"So far, most politicians in both parties have followed Charlie Brown's advice: 'No problem is so big that it can't be run away from.' "

-1984 letter

* * *

"Writing checks to the IRS that include strings of zeros does not bother Charlie or me. Berkshire as a corporation, and we as individuals, have prospered in America as we would have in no other country. Indeed, if we lived in some other part of the world and completely escaped taxes, I'm sure we would be worse off financially (and in many other ways as well). Overall, we feel extraordinarily lucky to have been dealt a hand in life that enables us to write large checks to the government rather than one requiring the government to regularly write checks to us -- say, because we are disabled or unemployed."

-1998 letter

Uncategorized

"No matter how great the talent or effort, some things just take time: you can't produce a baby in one month by getting nine women pregnant."

-1985 letter

* * *

"Lester Maddox, when Governor of Georgia, was criticized regarding the state's abysmal prison system. 'The solution', he said, 'is simple. All we need is a better class of prisoners.' "

-1985 letter

* * *

"For you chocaholics who like to fantasize, one statistic: we (at subsidiary See's Candy) sell over 12,000 tons annually."

-1986 letter

"While the Kirby (vacuum cleaner) product is more expensive than most cleaners, it performs in a manner that leaves cheaper units far behind ('in the dust,' so to speak)."

-1986 letter

* * *

"The most important thing to do when you find yourself in a hole is to stop digging."

-1990 letter

* * *

"The fat lady has yet to gargle, let alone sing, and we won't know our true 1967 - 1990 cost of funds (from insurance premiums that the company has received, but hasn't yet had to pay all losses from) until all losses from this period have been settled many decades from now."

-1990 letter

* * *

"Ultimately, even the most optimistic manager must face reality."

-1992 letter

"It's only when the tide goes out that you learn who's been swimming naked."

-1992 letter

* * *

"There's no use running if you're on the wrong road."

-1993 letter

* * *

"Why must bands play as if they will be paid by the decibel?"

-1996 letter

* * *

"Inverting really works: Try singing country western songs backwards and you will quickly regain your house, your car and your wife."

-1996 letter

* * *

"I was recently studying the 1896 report of
Coke (and you think that you are behind in
your reading!)."

-1996 letter

* * *

On whether or not to continue printing and mailing
quarterly shareholder reports:

"...a small number (of Berkshire
shareholders) who want the quarterly
information have no interest in getting it off
the Internet. Being a life-long sufferer from
technophobia, I can empathize with this
group."

-1997 letter

* * *

"W. C. Fields once said, 'It was a woman
who drove me to drink, but unfortunately I
never had the chance to thank her.' "

-1999 letter

* * *

"In apparel, Fruit of the Loom increased
unit sales by 10 million dozen, or 14%, with
shipments of intimate apparel for women

and girls growing by 31%. Charlie, who is far more knowledgeable than I am on this subject, assures me that women are not wearing more underwear. With this expert input, I can only conclude that our market share in the women's category must be growing rapidly."

-2004 letter

* * *

"Patrick Wolff, twice US chess champion, will again be in the mall playing blindfolded against all comers. He tells me that he has never tried to play more than four games simultaneously while handicapped this way but might try to bump that limit to five or six this year. If you're a chess fan, take Patrick on -- but be sure to check his blindfold before your first move."

-1999 letter

* * *

"After two hours of give-and-take, (a group of finance students from the University of Tennessee who meet with Buffett), traditionally presents me with a thank-you gift. (The doors stay locked until they do.)"

-2003 letter

"Long ago, Mark Twain said: 'A man who tries to carry a cat home by its tail will learn a lesson that can be learned in no other way.' "

-2005 letter

* * *

"Over the years, a number of very smart people have learned the hard way that a long string of impressive numbers multiplied by a single zero always equals zero."

-2005 letter

* * *

"As we view GEICO's current opportunities, Tony and I feel like two hungry mosquitoes in a nudist camp. Juicy targets are everywhere."

-2008 letter

* * *

"A promise is no better than the person or institution making it."

-2008 letter

* * *

"It's often useful in testing a theory to push it to extremes."

-2008 letter

* * *

"Money will always flow toward opportunity, and there is an abundance of that in America. Commentators today often talk of 'great uncertainty.' But think back, for example, to December 6, 1941, October 18, 1987 and September 10, 2001. No matter how serene today may be, tomorrow is always uncertain.

Don't let that reality spook you. Throughout my lifetime, politicians and pundits have constantly moaned about terrifying problems facing America. Yet our citizens now live an astonishing six times better than when I was born. The prophets of doom have overlooked the all-important factor that is certain: Human potential is far from exhausted, and the American system for unleashing that potential – a system that has worked wonders for over two centuries despite frequent interruptions for recessions and even a Civil War – remains alive and effective.

We are not natively smarter than we were when our country was founded nor do we work harder. But look around you and see a world beyond the dreams of any colonial citizen. Now, as in 1776, 1861, 1932 and 1941, America's best days lie ahead."

-2010 letter

* * *

"Nevertheless, our views regarding long-term inflationary trends are as negative as ever. Like virginity, a stable price level seems capable of maintenance, but not of restoration."

-1981 letter

* * *

"...the most elusive of human goals - keeping things simple and remembering what you set out to do."

-1982 letter

* * *

"The rear-view mirror is always clearer than the windshield."

-1991 letter

* * *

"(Burlesque dancer) Gypsy Rose Lee
announced on one of her later birthdays: 'I
have everything I had last year; it's just that
it's all two inches lower.' "

-1987 letter

* * *

"Most people, no matter how sophisticated
they are in other matters, feel like babes in
the woods when purchasing jewelry. They
can judge neither quality nor price. For
them only one rule makes sense: If you don't
know jewelry, know the jeweler."

-1988 letter

* * *

"Marrying for money - a mistake under
most circumstances, (is) insanity if one is
already rich."

-1989 letter

* * *

"I tell the newcomers the story of the Tennessee group (of business students who were well-rewarded for their suggestion of Clayton Homes as an acquisition target, which Berkshire was very pleased to quickly act upon). I do this in the spirit of the farmer who enters his hen house with an ostrich egg and admonishes the flock: 'I don't like to complain, girls, but this is just a small sample of what the competition is doing.' To date, our new scouts have not brought us deals. But their mission in life has been made clear to them."

-2004 letter

* * *

"Kelly Muchemore, the Flo Ziegfeld of Berkshire, put on a magnificent shopping extravaganza last year, and she says that was just a warm-up for this year. (Kelly, I am delighted to report, is getting married in October. I'm giving her away and suggested that she make a little history by holding the wedding at the annual meeting. She balked, however, when Charlie insisted that he be the ringbearer.)"

-2004 letter

* * *

"Kelly Broz (neé Muchemore), the Flo Ziegfeld of Berkshire, ... got married in October, and I gave her away. She asked me how I wanted to be listed in the wedding program. I replied 'envious of the groom,' and that's the way it went to press."

-2005 letter

* * *

On the Chinese language edition of Poor Charlie's Almanack, the ever-popular book about Mr. Buffett's partner, Charlie Munger:

"So what if you can't read Chinese? Just buy a copy and carry it around; it will make you look urbane and erudite."

-2010 letter

* * *

"As one investor said in 2009 (regarding the effects of the Financial Crisis): 'This is worse than divorce. I've lost half my net worth – and I still have my wife.' "

-2010 letter

* * *

The Annual Shareholders' Meeting

It's estimated that up to 40,000 people attended Berkshire's annual shareholder meeting, which is billed by Mr. Buffett as Woodstock for Capitalists.

He also strongly urges attendees to open their wallets:

> "The best reason to exit (the official shareholder meeting), of course, is to shop. We will help you do that by filling the 194,300-square foot hall that adjoins the meeting area with products from dozens of Berkshire subsidiaries. Last year, you did your part, and most locations racked up

record sales. In a nine-hour period, we sold 1,053 pairs of Justin boots, 12,416 pounds of See's candy, 8,000 Dairy Queen Blizzards® and 8,800 Quikut knives (that's 16 knives per minute). But you can do better. Remember: Anyone who says money can't buy happiness simply hasn't learned where to shop."

-2008 letter

* * *

"Our capitalist's version of Woodstock - the Berkshire Annual Meeting - will be held on Monday, May 5. Charlie and I thoroughly enjoy this event, and we hope that you come. We will start at 9:30 a.m., break for about 15 minutes at noon (food will be available - but at a price, of course), and then continue talking to hard-core attendees until at least 3:30."

-1996 letter

* * *

On a "crisis" at the 1996 annual shareholder meeting:

"The night before the meeting, I lost my voice, thereby fulfilling Charlie's wildest fantasy. He was crushed when I showed up the next morning with my speech restored."

-1997 letter

* * *

"Borsheim's (jewelry) normally is closed on Sunday, but we will open for shareholders and their guests from noon to 6 p.m. ... At our Sunday opening last year you made Ike very happy: After totaling the day's volume, he suggested to me that we start holding annual meetings quarterly."

-1990 letter

* * *

"The piece de resistance of our one-company trade show will be a 79-foot-long, nearly 12-foot-wide, fully-outfitted cabin of a 737 Boeing Business Jet ("BBJ"), which is NetJets' newest product. This plane has a 14-hour range; is designed to carry 19 passengers; and offers a bedroom, an office, and two showers. ...The BBJ will be available for your inspection on May 1-3 near the entrance … Bring along your checkbook in case you decide to make an impulse purchase."

-1998 letter

* * *

"Come to Omaha by bus; leave in your new plane. And take along – with no fear of a strip search – the Ginsu knives that you've purchased at the exhibit of our Quikut subsidiary."

-2008 letter

* * *

"In recent years … there has been a mad rush when the doors open at 7 a.m., led by people who wish to be first in line at the 12 microphones available for questioners. This is not desirable from a safety standpoint, nor do we believe that sprinting ability should be the determinant of who gets to pose questions. (At age 78, I've concluded that speed afoot is a ridiculously overrated talent.)"

-2008 letter

* * *

"Nicholas Kenner nailed me - again - at last year's meeting, pointing out that I had said in the 1990 annual report that he was 11 in May 1990, when actually he was 9. So, asked Nicholas rather caustically: 'If you can't get that straight, how do I know the numbers in the back - the financials - are correct?' I'm still searching for a snappy response. Nicholas will be at this year's meeting - he spurned my offer of a trip to Disney World on that day - so join us to watch a continuation of this lop-sided battle of wits."

-1991 letter

* * *

"Last year in this report, I described my family's delight with the one-quarter (200 flight hours annually) of a Hawker 1000 that we had owned since 1995. I got so pumped up by my own prose that shortly thereafter I signed up for one-sixteenth of a Cessna V Ultra as well. Now my annual outlays at (subsidiary Executive Jet Aviation, which sells and manages the fractional ownership of jet aircraft, through its NetJets® program) and Borsheim's (subsidiary jewelry retailer), combined, total ten times my salary. Think of this as a rough guideline for your own expenditures with us."

-1999 letter

* * *

"After a short recess, Charlie and I will convene the (Berkshire shareholders') annual meeting at 3:15. If you decide to leave during the day's question periods, please do so while Charlie is talking."

-2006 letter

* * *

"Our special treat for shareholders this year will be the return of my friend, Ariel Hsing, the country's top-ranked junior table tennis player (and a good bet to win at the Olympics some day). Now 14, Ariel came to the annual meeting four years ago and demolished all comers, including me. (You can witness my humiliating defeat on YouTube; just type in Ariel Hsing Berkshire.)

Naturally, I've been plotting a comeback and will take her on outside of Borsheims at 1:00 p.m. on Sunday. It will be a three-point match, and after I soften her up, all shareholders are invited to try their luck at similar three-point contests. Winners will be

given a box of See's candy. We will have
equipment available, but bring your own
paddle if you think it will help. (It won't.)"

-2009 letter

Indeed, Ms. Hsing has since won the following 2011 US National Championships: Women's Singles, Mixed Doubles and 21 & Under Women's Singles. She was born in 1995, which makes her a bit younger than most of my underwear.

* * *

Baseball Anyone?

Mr. Buffett could give a fine seminar on trash-talking...

"Opening the (Omaha Royals baseball)
game that night, I had my stuff and threw a
strike that the scoreboard reported at eight
miles per hour. What many fans missed was
that I shook off the catcher's call for my fast
ball and instead delivered my change-up.
This year it will be all smoke."

-1994 letter

* * *

"On Saturday evening, May 4, there will be a baseball game at Rosenblatt Stadium between the Omaha Royals and the Louisville Redbirds. I expect to make the opening pitch - owning a quarter of the team assures me of one start per year - but our manager, Mike Jirschele, will probably make his usual mistake and yank me immediately after. About 1,700 shareholders attended last year's game. Unfortunately, we had a rain-out, which greatly disappointed the many scouts in the stands. But the smart ones will be back this year, and I plan to show them my best stuff."

-1995 letter

* * *

"The (partly Buffett-owned) Omaha Royals and Indianapolis Indians will play baseball on Saturday evening, May 3rd, at Rosenblatt Stadium. Pitching in my normal rotation - one throw a year - I will start.

Though Rosenblatt is normal in appearance, it is anything but: The field sits on a unique geological structure that occasionally emits short gravitational waves causing even the most smoothly-delivered pitch to sink violently. I have been the victim of this weird phenomenon several times in the past but am hoping for benign conditions this year. There will be lots of opportunities for photos at the ball game, but you will need incredibly fast reflexes to snap my fast ball en route to the plate."

-1996 letter

* * *

"The Omaha Royals and Albuquerque Dukes will play baseball on Saturday evening, May 2nd, at Rosenblatt Stadium. As usual, your Chairman, shamelessly exploiting his 25% ownership of the team, will take the mound. But this year you will see something new.

In past games, much to the bafflement of the crowd, I have shaken off the catcher's first call. He has consistently asked for my sweeping curve, and I have just as regularly resisted. Instead, I have served up a pathetic fast ball, which on my best day was clocked at eight miles per hour (with a following wind).

There's a story behind my unwillingness to throw the curve ball. As some of you may know, Candy Cummings invented the curve in 1867 and used it to great effect in the National Association, where he never won less than 28 games in a season. The pitch, however, drew immediate criticism from the very highest of authorities, namely Charles

Elliott, then president of Harvard University, who declared, 'I have heard that this year we at Harvard won the baseball championship because we have a pitcher who has a fine curve ball. I am further instructed that the purpose of the curve ball is to deliberately deceive the batter. Harvard is not in the business of teaching deception.' (I'm not making this up.)

Ever since I learned of President Elliott's moral teachings on this subject, I have scrupulously refrained from using my curve, however devastating its effect might have been on hapless batters. Now, however, it is time for my karma to run over Elliott's dogma and for me to quit holding back. Visit the park on Saturday night and marvel at the majestic arc of my breaking ball."

-1997 letter

* * *

"The Omaha Golden Spikes (neé the Omaha Royals) will meet the Iowa Cubs on Saturday evening, May 1st, at Rosenblatt Stadium. Your Chairman, whose breaking ball had the crowd buzzing last year, will again take the mound. This year I plan to introduce my 'flutterball.' It's a real source of irritation to me that many view our annual meeting as a financial event rather than the sports classic I consider it to be. Once the world sees my flutterball, that misperception will be erased."

-1998 letter

* * *

"The usual baseball game will be held at Rosenblatt Stadium at 7 p.m. on Saturday night. This year the Omaha Golden Spikes will play the Iowa Cubs. Come early, because that's when the real action takes place. Those who attended last year saw your Chairman pitch to Ernie Banks.

This encounter proved to be the titanic duel that the sports world had long awaited. After the first few pitches -- which were not my best, but when have I ever thrown my best? -- I fired a brushback at Ernie just to let him know who was in command. Ernie charged the mound, and I charged the plate. But a clash was avoided because we became exhausted before reaching each other.

Ernie was dissatisfied with his performance last year and has been studying the game films all winter. As you may know, Ernie had 512 home runs in his career as a Cub. Now that he has spotted telltale weaknesses in my delivery, he expects to get #513 on April 29. I, however, have learned new ways to disguise my "flutterball." Come and watch this matchup.

I should add that I have extracted a promise from Ernie that he will not hit a "come-backer" at me since I would never be able to duck in time to avoid it. My reflexes are like Woody Allen's, who said his were so slow that he was once hit by a car being pushed by two guys."

-1999 letter

* * *

"The usual baseball game will be held at Rosenblatt Stadium at 7 p.m. on Saturday night. This year the Omaha Golden Spikes will play the New Orleans Zephyrs. Ernie Banks is again going to be on hand to - bravely - face my fastball (once clocked at 95 mpm - miles per month).

My performance last year was not my best: It took me five pitches to throw anything resembling a strike. And, believe me, it gets lonely on the mound when you can't find the plate. Finally, I got one over, and Ernie lashed a line drive to left field. After I was yanked from the game, the many sports writers present asked what I had served up to Ernie. I quoted what Warren Spahn said after Willie Mays hit one of his pitches for a home run (Willie's first in the majors): 'It was a helluva pitch for the first sixty feet.'

It will be a different story this year. I don't want to tip my hand, so let's just say Ernie will have to deal with a pitch he has never seen before."

-2000 letter

* * *

"The usual baseball game will be held at Rosenblatt Stadium at 7 p.m. on Saturday night. This year the Omaha Royals will play the Oklahoma RedHawks. Last year, in an attempt to emulate the career switch of Babe Ruth, I gave up pitching and tried batting. Bob Gibson, an Omaha native, was on the mound and I was terrified, fearing Bob's famous brush-back pitch. Instead, he delivered a fast ball in the strike zone, and with a Mark McGwire-like swing, I managed to connect for a hard grounder, which inexplicably died in the infield. I didn't run it out: At my age, I get winded playing a hand of bridge.

I'm not sure what will take place at the ballpark this year, but come out and be surprised. Our proxy statement contains instructions for obtaining tickets to the game. Those people ordering tickets to the annual meeting will receive a booklet containing all manner of information that should help you enjoy your visit in Omaha. There will be plenty of action in town. So come for Woodstock Weekend and join our Celebration of Capitalism at the Civic."

-2001 letter

* * *

"There won't be a ball game this year. After my fastball was clocked at 5 mph last year, I decided to hang up my spikes. "

-2002 letter

* * *

The Last Word

Working on this book has been a very enjoyable education and I would like to convey my sincere thanks to Mr. Buffett for generously authorizing the use of his copyrighted material.

While I'm sure he's not a saint, he's probably as close as any Fortune 500 senior executive has ever been.

Hats off to his wit, wisdom and leadership style!

ALSO BY MARK GAVAGAN

12 Critical Things Your Family Needs to Know

The It's All Right Here Life & Affairs Organizer

These are print/digital workbooks for helping families organize their finances and get their affairs in order, so that if something happens to you, your loved ones will know:

- What you have

- Where it's located, and

- What your wishes are

Learn more at:

www.OrganizeMyAffairs.com

Made in the USA
San Bernardino, CA
21 June 2014